My name is

Quintin

This book is a gift from

My Mom + Dad

The first song I remember singing is

Here I am to Worship

2012 First Printing

Copyright © 2012 by Paraclete Press, Inc.

ISBN 978-1-55725-911-0

Acknowledgments:
"Jesus Loves Me" text by Anna B. Warner
"All Things Bright and Beautiful" text by Cecil Frances Alexander
"I've Got the Joy" originally written by George Willis Cooke
"This is My Father's World" text by Maltbie D. Babcock
"Go Tell It on the Mountain" author unknown, traditional African-American spiritual
"Fairest Lord Jesus" text by Munster Gesangbuch; translation by Joseph August Seiss
"What a Friend We Have in Jesus" text by Joseph M. Scriven
"I Sing a Song of the Saints of God" text by Lesbia Scott
"He's Got the Whole World in His Hands" author unknown, traditional American spiritual
"When We All Get to Heaven" text by Eliza E. Hewitt

10 9 8 7 6 5 4 3 2 1

Published by Paraclete Press
Brewster, Massachusetts
www.paracletepress.com
Printed in Singapore

MY FIRST HYMN BOOK

Clare Simpson

PARACLETE PRESS

Brewster, Massachusetts

Contents

6

I
love
to sing.

God must love singing—

because there is so much singing in the Bible!

Heavenly angels sing.

8

King David loved to sing.

"Sing to the Lord a new song," David said.
"Let the oceans roar, the rivers clap, and the
mountains sing for joy!"

Mary, the blessed mother of Jesus,

sang a famous song.

My soul proclaims the greatness of the Lord

And *you* can sing, too!

13

Jesus Loves Me!

Jesus loves me! This I know,

For the Bible tells me so.

Little ones to Him belong;

They are weak, but He is strong.

Yes, Jesus loves me!

Yes, Jesus loves me!

Yes, Jesus loves me!

The Bible tells me so.

Jesus loves me! This I know,

As He loved so long ago,

Taking children on His knee,

Saying, "Let them come to Me."

Yes, Jesus loves me!

Yes, Jesus loves me!

Yes, Jesus loves me!

The Bible tells me so.

Jesus loves me still today,
Walking with me on my way,
Wanting as a friend to give
Light and love to all who live.

Yes, Jesus loves me!

Yes, Jesus loves me!

Yes, Jesus loves me!

The Bible tells me so.

The World Around Me

All Things Bright and Beautiful

All things bright and beautiful,

All creatures great and small,

All things wise and wonderful:

The Lord God made them all.

Each little flower that opens,
Each little bird that sings,
God made their glowing colors,
And made their tiny wings.

The purple-headed mountains,
The river running by,
The sunset and the morning
That brightens up the sky.

The cold wind in the winter,

The pleasant summer sun,

The ripe fruits in the garden:

God made them every one.

God gave us eyes to see them,

And lips that we might tell

How great is God Almighty,

Who has made all things well.

I've Got the Joy

I've got the joy, joy, joy, joy

Down in my heart (Where?)

Down in my heart (Where?)

Down in my heart

I've got the joy, joy, joy, joy

Down in my heart (Where?)

Down in my heart to stay.

I've got the peace that passes understanding Down in my heart (Where?)

Down in my heart (Where?)

Down in my heart

I've got the peace that passes understanding

Down in my heart (Where?)

Down in my heart to stay.

Well, if the devil doesn't like it
he can sit on a tack! (Ouch!)
Sit on a tack! (Ouch!)
  Sit on a tack!

Well, if the devil doesn't like it
he can sit on a tack! (Ouch!)
  Sit on a tack to stay.

God

This Is My Father's World

This is my Father's world,
And to my listening ears all nature sings,
And round me rings
The music of the spheres.

This is my Father's world:
I rest me in the thought of rocks and trees,
Of skies and seas;
His hand the wonders wrought.

This is my Father's world,
The birds their carols raise,
The morning light, the lily white,
Declare their Maker's praise.

This is my Father's world,
He shines in all that's fair;
In the rustling grass I hear Him pass;
He speaks to me everywhere.

This is my Father's world:

Why should my heart be sad?

The Lord is King; let the heavens ring!

God reigns; let the earth be glad!

Jesus

34

Go Tell It on the Mountain

Go, tell it on the mountain,

Over the hills and everywhere

Go, tell it on the mountain,

That Jesus Christ is born.

While shepherds kept their watching

O'er silent flocks by night,

Behold, throughout the heavens

There shone a holy light.

The shepherds feared and trembled,

When lo! above the earth,

Rang out the angels chorus

That hailed our Savior's birth.

Down in a lowly manger
The humble Christ was born
And God sent us salvation
That blessed Christmas morn.

Go, tell it on the mountain,
Over the hills and everywhere
Go, tell it on the mountain,
That Jesus Christ is born.

39

Fairest Lord Jesus

Fairest Lord Jesus,

Ruler of all nature,

O thou of God and man the Son,

Thee will I cherish, Thee will I honor,

Thou, my soul's glory, joy, and crown.

Fair are the meadows,
Fairer still the woodlands,
Robed in the blooming garb of spring:
Jesus is fairer, Jesus is purer
Who makes the woeful heart to sing.

Fair is the sunshine,

Fairer still the moonlight,

And all the twinkling starry host:

Jesus shines brighter, Jesus shines purer

Than all the angels heaven can boast.

What a Friend We Have in Jesus

What a Friend we have in Jesus,
all our sins and griefs to bear!
What a privilege to carry everything
to God in prayer!
O what peace we often forfeit,
O what needless pain we bear,
All because we do not carry
everything to God in prayer.

Have we trials and temptations?
Is there trouble anywhere?
We should never be discouraged;
take it to the Lord in prayer.
Can we find a friend so faithful
who will all our sorrows share?
Jesus knows our every weakness;
take it to the Lord in prayer.

45

Saints

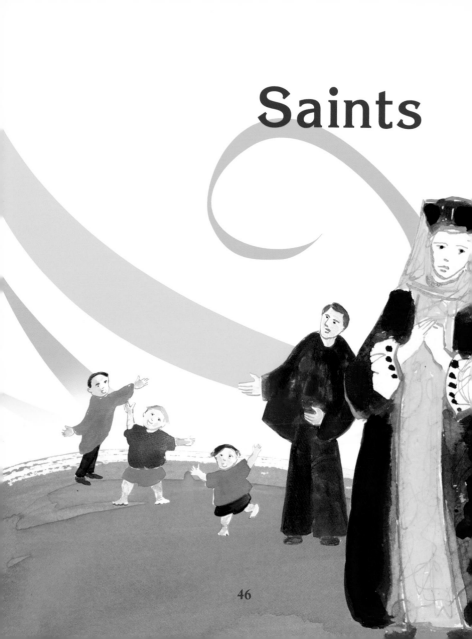

I Sing a Song of the Saints of God

I sing a song of the saints of God,
   patient and brave and true,
   who toiled and fought and lived and died
   for the Lord they loved and knew.
And one was a doctor, and one was a queen,
   and one was a shepherdess on the green;
   they were all of them saints of God,
   and I mean, God helping, to be one too.

They loved their Lord so dear, so dear,
and His love made them strong;
and they followed the right for Jesus' sake
the whole of their good lives long.
And one was a soldier, and one was a priest,
and one was slain by a fierce wild beast;
and there's not any reason,
no, not the least, why I shouldn't be one too.

They lived not only in ages past;

there are hundreds of thousands still.

The world is bright with the joyous saints

who love to do Jesus' will.

You can meet them in school, on the street, in the store,

in church, by the sea, in the house next door;

they are saints of God, whether rich or poor,

and I mean to be one too.

Forever

He's Got the Whole World in His Hands

He's got the whole world in His hands,

He's got the whole world in His hands,

He's got the whole world in His hands,

He's got the whole world in His hands.

He's got the wind and the rain in His hands,

He's got the wind and the rain in His hands,

He's got the wind and the rain in His hands,

He's got the whole world in His hands.

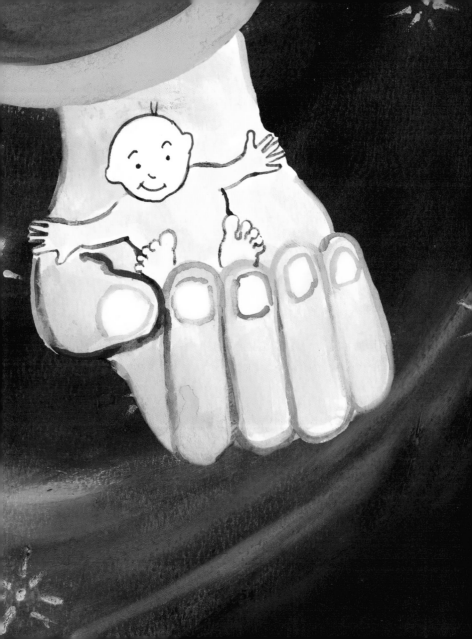

He's got the tiny little baby in His hands,
He's got the tiny little baby in His hands,
He's got the tiny little baby in His hands,
He's got the whole world in His hands.

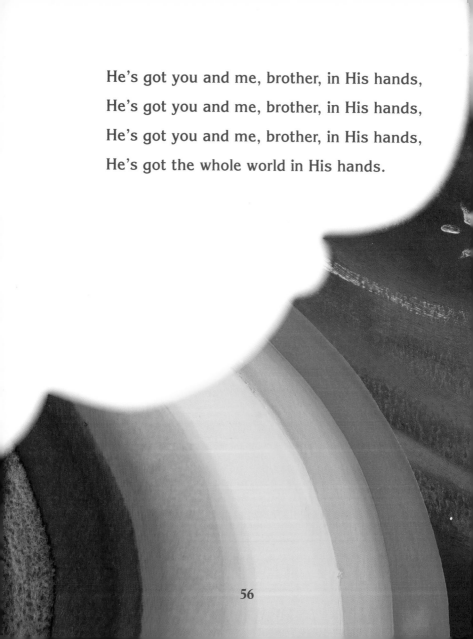

He's got you and me, brother, in His hands,

He's got you and me, brother, in His hands,

He's got you and me, brother, in His hands,

He's got the whole world in His hands.

The B-I-B-L-E

The B-I-B-L-E, yes that's the book for me.

I stand alone on the word of God

The B-I-B-L-E!

The B-I-B-L-E, yes that's the book for me.

I stand alone on the word of God

The B-I-B-L-E!

When We All Get to Heaven

When we all get to heaven,

What a day of rejoicing that will be!

When we all see Jesus,

We'll sing and shout the victory!

Onward to the prize before us!

Soon His beauty we'll behold;

Soon the pearly gates will open;

We shall tread the streets of gold.